THE VILLAGE SCHOOL

John Vince

SORBUS

CONTENTS

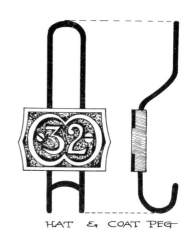

HAT & COAT PEG

ACKNOWLEDGEMENTS.

The author thanks the following for their help. Jayne Cartwright, Major H.T.K. Phillips, M. Arnold, George Lamb, Jo Lawrie, Wynne Frankum, Acton Scott Farm, Katesgrove Schoolroom, Northampton Library, Bucks County Museum, Uffington Museum, Sevington School.

ISBN 1 874329 60 5

Introduction

The first schools for village children date from the C17. Buildings were given or money donated to start these early schools which often had limited numbers of pupils.

A large number of schools were set up in the C18 sponsored by the S.P.C.K. In the C19 British and National schools added to these early foundations. The first local government schools, BOARD schools, were established in the 1870s.

School work in the C19 largely concentrated upon a child's memory. The 3R's were mastered by a process of formal drills, & failure to learn often resulted in physical punishment. From 1861 a system of payment by results was imposed & this lasted for about thirty years before it was abandoned. This book describes the different kinds of school & illustrates some of the furniture & equipment once considered essential for a child's learning. For many children school life in the C19 was endured rather than enjoyed.

A·FREE·SCHOOLE·FOR
WEEKLEY·AND·WERCKTON
FOVNDED·BY·NICOLAS·LATHAM
CLERKE·PARSON·OF·BARNEWELL
S·ANDREW·TO·TEACH·T·HEIRE
CHILDREN·TO·WRIT·E·AND·READE
ANNO·DOMINI·1624

Charity Schools

IMMANUEL.
For ȳ training up of
poor Children in
good morality, & a
Reverent, Orthodox
Piety in a Conſtant
Keeping ȳ Church
& in all Sorts of ȳ
Beſt Learning, this
BIBLE-School was
founded & Endowd
by Rich. Hill. B. D.
Rector. 1715.
GLORY BE TO GOD

Long before there was any organised system of schooling certain people realised the importance of education. Sometimes an individual financed the building of a school for a parish. Other schools were founded by endowments. In some places a school was built but no funds were given for a teacher. When other donors provided money for teaching such schools could begin to operate.

There are many village schools which were built in the C17 or earlier. The splendid village school at Ewelme, Oxon. was built in 1435, when Henry VI was King, & it is still open. Few records survive from these early schools so we do not know exactly how they functioned.

The school, c.1700, at Great Linford, Bucks. is set between almshouses.

Ɵ THURCASTON, LEICS.

4

Most of the early parish schools were used on Sundays to teach the Bible & reading. If a schoolmaster was appointed to a day-school the scholars, usually boys, would be taught reading, writing & arithmetic - often called 'casting accounts.'

In 1698 the SOCIETY for PROMOTING CHRISTIAN KNOWLEDGE (S.P.C.K) was formed. Its purpose was to spread the Gospel abroad & to establish schools for poor children in Britain. Before parishes had a school the nave of the parish church was often used as a schoolroom.

Billesdon School, Leics. (c.1650)

Top: Uffington, Oxon. 1617.

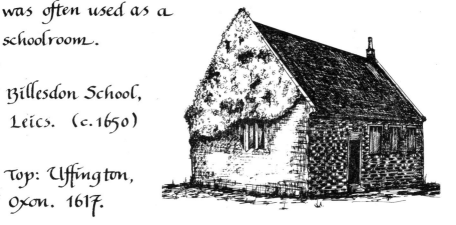

British Schools

Joseph Lancaster, a Quaker, founded the Lancastrian Society in 1808 to allow him to put his educational ideas into practice. He used a system of teaching which allowed one teacher to control up to a hundred children. The teacher had a number of MONITORS who each had to oversee the work of a group of other pupils (a division). Monitors were the older scholars but they could be as young as twelve years. The advantage of the monitorial system was its low cost. After the school day was over the monitors received lessons from the teacher to prepare for the next day.

Most of the schoolwork was presented in small sections; such as a set of spellings or a multiplication table which children had to learn by heart (rote).

In 1810 the Lancastrian Society changed its name to the British & Foreign Schools Society. Schools were established in many villages & mostly attracted pupils from non-conformist families. In some places British & National schools competed for pupils.

These rules show us how good conduct was emphasised in Victorian schools. Church schools had very similar expectations. The importance of regular attendance (Rule 1) should be noted. It must have been difficult for some pupils to comply adequately with Rule 2 when all

RULES OF BRITISH SCHOOL

1 To attend School constantly at Nine in the Morning and Two in the Afternoon.

2 To attend School with Hands and Face clean, Hair combed and Shoes brushed.

3 On all occasions to speak the Truth.

4 To behave with particular and solemn reverent Quietness when reading Holy Scriptures.

5 to behave with Solemnity in all Places of Public Worship.

6 To avoid all bad Company.

8 Never use bad Words or ill Names.

9 To avoid all Quarrelling and Contention.

10 Never to mock lame or deformed Persons and to be kind to all men.

11 to avoid Cruelty, and never teaze or in any way harm brute Creatures.

12 To be silent in School.

13 To enter and leave School orderly.

14 To obey the Rules and Orders of the School.

Whenever a boy is about to leave School, it is expected he will inform the Master.

domestic water came from a well or outdoor pump. Rules 3, 10 & 11 remind us that schools also accepted responsibility for setting moral standards.

National Schools

LANGLEY BURRELL · WILTS

The 'National Society for the Education of the Poor in the Principles of the Established Church' was founded in 1811. It helped the development of Church of England schools by giving grants to assist building projects & to pay for teaching staff. The schools it supported became known as 'National Schools'. Earlier foundations sponsored by the S.P.C.K. became part of the scheme. In most of the National schools the monitorial system, derived from the Lancastrian model, continued to be used.

In C.of E. schools the vicar usually visited each week, rehearsed children in the Catechism & conducted prayers. Once a year the children were examined in Religious Knowledge by the Diocesan Inspector.

On some saints' days children went to church in the morning & perhaps enjoyed a holiday afterwards. The main school holiday took place in the summer. This was known as the Harvest Holiday and its timing changed from year to year depending upon the ripening of the crops. Log books record the Harvest Holiday taking place at any time from July to late September. Although children were not at school they had to work in the harvest field.

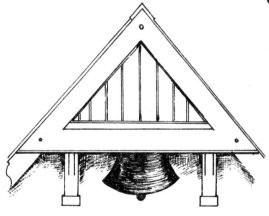

Some schools had an outside bell in a turret or attached to a gable end. This bell could be heard all over the village & so children knew when it was time to go to school. Many people in Victorian times did not have a household clock. The bell monitor had to ring the bell before the start of morning school & again in the afternoon. Lateness was often punished & many children reached the classroom out of breath.

Board Schools

Board Schools were established following the Forster Education Act 1870. This Act divided England into districts. Each county had a number of districts & each district was managed by a Board. Some school boards administered several schools. BOARD SCHOOLS were the first local authority schools. They were set up in places where school provision was insufficient. Board schools were undenominational. They did not have to provide religious education but the 1870 Act 'permitted' them to do so.

The typical Board School is constructed of brick & has a slated roof. These were the cheapest & most readily available materials at that time. Windows were placed high up so that pupils could not look out and become distracted from their work.

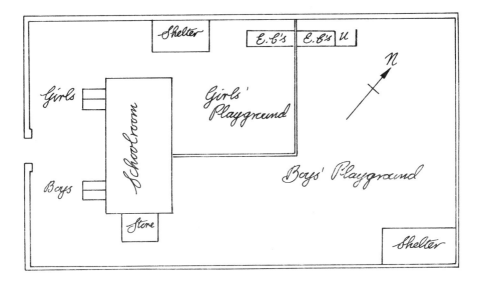

PLAYGROUNDS & entrances were often separated so that boys & girls used different areas. Some playgrounds had covered shelters so that pupils had a dry place in wet weather.

The attitude of adults towards 'rough' games is shown by a passage in the 'Child's First Book' - c.1848 - which contains the following advice:

'To play at football is dangerous. I advise every good boy to avoid such a rough game, if he wishes to have his legs & feet kept from injury.'

'Boys like marbles to play with. But it is hurtful to throw them at each other, as some boys will do when they are not pleased.'

The impact of such exhortation on young readers is not known!

Council Schools

The Balfour Education Act in 1902 made local authorities responsible for providing elementary & secondary education. District & county councils absorbed and replaced the Board School system. Under this Act some 'districts' were quite small & provided education for a single town. The 1944 Education Act abolished these smaller districts & each county became responsible for the schools within its boundaries. The 'church' voluntary schools also became part of the country-wide system, but they retained their separate status in matters concerning religious education. There are still two types of voluntary school - 'Aided' schools have a majority of church governors & 'Controlled' schools have a majority of county governors.

STOKE MANDEVILLE COUNCIL SCHOOL

OFFICES

Every school had to provide essential 'offices' for its pupils. In the C19 earth closets were used, and in some schools this primitive system was still in operation in the 1940s! The change to water closets came about gradually as villages aquired a mains supply. The offices had always been placed as far away from the schoolroom as possible. After water closets came into use the exposed location of the buildings led to freezing up & burst pipes.

A school manual - of 1885 - advises that 'The offices for the boys & girls must be completely out of hearing & should be out of sight of one another. Objectionable writing is more likely to occur here than in any other part of the premises. This may almost entirely be prevented by good supervision.'

Thomas Hardy - THE·RETURN·OF·THE·NATIVE - was familiar with 'bad words' on gates & barns:

'If they'd never been taught to write they wouldn't have been able to scribble such villainy.'

Schoolwork

~STANDARDS~

From 1861 a school inspector visited the school each year to examine the children's work. This system, revised in 1862, had seven 'standards'. Its object was to make sure that schools received grant payments based on the pupils' results. The examination tested reading, writing & arithmetic - the 3 R's.

Standard I -7yrs- required the child to :(a) read a narrative in monosyllables; (b) form on a slate, by dictation, figures up to 20 & add/subtract figures up to 19 ;(c) form on a slate by dictation capital & small letters. Standard VI -12yrs- expected (a) reading a paragraph from a newspaper; (b) complete the sum of a bill; (c) complete a newspaper paragraph by dictation.

If the pupils' performance was poor in an examination the amount of grant would be reduced & so would the teacher's salary.

In 1890 these financial arrangements were abandoned & replaced by grants for 'attendance, discipline and organisation'.

The payments by results scheme had not worked!

THE TIMETABLE

School time tables were very rigid & formal as this example shows.

A.M.

9.15-9.30 ~ Registration. Examination of hands and shoes. Prayers with Lesson

9.30-10.00 ~ Tables by rote, followed by formal Scripture

10.00-10.30 ~ Arithmetic from blackboard. Attention to layout, figure formation and correction of errors

10.30-10.45 ~   Playtime

10.45-11.15 ~   Music Practice Shepherd songs, Songs of the Empire.

11.15-12.00 ~ Cursive Writing Practice from copybooks - Letter to an employer.

12.00   Dinner time

P.M.

1.15-2.30 ~ Object Lesson - The Giraffe Playground Drill - if wet History of India

2.30-2.40 ~ Playtime

2.40-3.25 ~ Reading   Poetry Story - continue "The Water Babies"

3.30 ~   Prayers   Dismiss

January 1882

READING

One of the oldest forms of book is the HORN BOOK which was still in use in the C19. This two-sided book had its writing covered with a sheet of thin horn to protect the text. Horn books usually displayed the alphabet & part of the Lord's Prayer.

READING set a person apart & opened up many opportunities for children from ordinary homes. Before attendance became compulsory, & probably after, some parents looked upon schooling as an unwanted imposition which prevented a child from working.

'What do our Alf want wi a lot of book larnin? He can read & write and add up as much money as he's ever likely to get. What more do he want?" FLORA THOMPSON 'LARK RISE TO CANDLEFORD'

Reading charts like this were repeated by a class in chorus as a monitor pointed to each line in turn.

WRITING

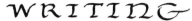

In the mediaeval period the ability to read & write was restricted to priests & some 'gentlemen'. By the C18 merchants & their servants had to be literate & able to 'cast accounts'. Slowly the need for clerks to keep written records developed & this was one reason for the creation of many Charity Schools in the Georgian period. Quills were the essential tools of the scribe until the development of the steel pen by Joseph Guillot, of Birmingham, in 1820. By 1845 quills had become obsolete'. In the old school at Dorchester, Oxon., now a museum, you can still see the quill drawers used by the scholars. Writing in school often began by making letter shapes in a sand tray with a stick. Slates were used for writing by younger pupils as this saved paper. Slate pencils were used for writing & they could make a disturbing 'squeak' if mis-used !

SAND TRAY

17

PEN WIPER.

Pens were used by older children. Many copy books were published and these provided models for written exercises. These were usually repetitive and dull. The long pointed nibs were designed to produce the 'copperplate' script. Thicker strokes were made by increasing pressure on the nib - a difficult skill for young hands to master.

INK was supplied in clay bottles, sometimes protected by wickerwork. Glass bottles eventually replaced clay. Aproned INK-MONITORS dispensed the ink in china wells. Early versions had open tops but later examples had a small central hole to keep out dust. Inkwells were carried in an inktray, but they were filled outside the classroom. Filled wells were distributed on Mondays & gathered for washing on Fridays. Pen wipers made from scraps of material also had non-writing uses!

INK·JUGS.

ARITHMETIC

Counting was the first stage of mastering numbers. As soon as they entered school, some as young as three years, pupils began the process of counting. Numbers were written in a sand tray or on a slate. A great deal of counting was done together. The monitor stood in front of the class & moved the coloured beads on the ABACUS as the pupils chanted the numbers. The abacus was one of the few pieces of apparatus a school possessed.

For many country people calculating was more important than reading. Pupils however had to be drilled in arithmetic in the same mechanical way as reading required. The 'tables' of multiplication (up to 12 times) measurement & weight had to be mastered. In the days when pounds, shillings & pence were used long multiplication & division presented many problems. What is the correct answer to this sum?

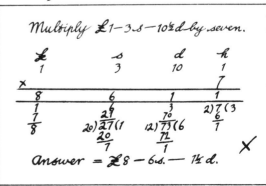

Multiply £1–3s–10½d by seven.

£	s	d	h
1	3	10	1
×			7
8	6	1	1
1	2/	3	2)7 (3
7	2/)27(1	12)73(6	6
8	20	72	7
	7	1	

Answer = £8 – 6s. — 1½ d.   ✗

CAN YOU FIND THE MISTAKE ?

19

~OBJECT LESSONS~

By the 1880s an important addition was made to the mechanical rote learning of reading, writing & arithmetic. This innovation was the OBJECT LESSON. These lessons made it possible for more informal discussion to take place. We must remember that most pupils came from poor homes & had little opportunity to experience anything beyond their immediate surroundings. The list of contents in "THE HANDY BOOK OF OBJECT LESSONS" · J. WALKER · 1885 · may not seem exciting to the C20 reader but they must have provided relief from a dull diet of endless repetition. The subjects included ~ Elephant, Lion, Tiger, Beaver, Llama, Rattle Snake, Tea, Chocolate Tree, Caoutchouc Tree, Gold, Salt, Chalk, Potato, Mahogany Tree, Sealing wax, Diving Bell. This apparent random choice of subjects may puzzle those used to a more systematic approach.

~EMPIRE DAY~

In 1902, on Queen Victoria's birthday - 24th. May, EMPIRE DAY was inaugurated. This was celebrated in the nation's schools & pupils were sometimes given a 'certificate' to mark their part in the proceedings. The day's events were arranged by individual schools, but notes of guidance were issued by some county councils. A typical programme was: MORNING

1. Hoist the Union Jack. 2. Sing the National Anthem. 3. Salute the flag & sing such patriotic songs as may be known. 4. Teachers give lessons suitable to the capacities of children on the history & growth of the British Empire. 5. Give history of Union Jack. 6. Children write a letter to the children of one of our Colonies, telling them of the life in their school or village. 7. Children or Teacher read or recite some poem illustrative of heroic duty & self sacrifice on behalf of the Nation. AFTERNOON - 8. Organised games under the supervision & instruction of the teachers. 9. National Anthem & final salute.

In some schools children had a holiday in the afternoon.

Empire Day was renamed Commonwealth Day in 1958.

21

Rewards

H. M. Inspector considers that, till quite recently, the measures taken by your Board for enforcing school attendance have been quite insufficient to attain their object, and that the attendance officer has not done his duty satisfactorily the result has been shewn in the very small number of children who have qualified

C.1880.

School log-books of the C19 contain many references to attendance. After 1890 part of the annual grant was given for regular attendance. There were many reasons for absence. Girls were often kept at home to look after new-born infants. Boys were frequently expected to work in the fields bird scaring, stone picking, at haytime & harvest. Lack of footwear also prevented children from walking long distances in bad weather. To encourage good attendance & conduct, medals were awarded each year.

The oldest medal the author has seen is dated 1896, but earlier specimens may exist. Some medals have a name on the face & others are engraved on the edge.

There are many different designs to be found. The NATIONAL SOCIETY produced a medal used by many church schools. Board schools, particularly in towns, struck their own medals and, after 1902, County Councils added to the list. The heads of King Edward VII & King George V, civic arms, landmarks & allegorical figures all feature on medals awarded for attendance.

'Bars' could be added to the ribbon to indicate a second or even third year of distinctive attendance. Medals were still awarded in Bedfordshire in the 1950s.

Bronze was often used for medals, some had a gilt finish & others were made from a light alloy.

Furniture

In the C17 & C18 scholars sat on benches. The desks which survive today, from the C19 onwards, are of two main types. I. single wooden desk with a fixed seat; II. benches which could seat two or more pupils. It is difficult to date desks exactly. The example [A] has a reversed curved splat [x] to make the user sit upright. Its locker with the lift-up lid could slide about 4" [←→y] to allow for the pupil's size. There is no inkwell & this may suggest that it was intended for a younger age group. Desks of this kind were made in several sizes. The bench B has no back to its fixed seat & a narrow shelf below the writing slope. This type of desk was often used on a gallery as it could seat several pupils in a small space.

BLACK COUNTRY MUSEUM, DUDLEY.

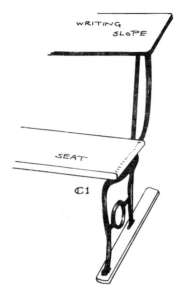

WRITING SLOPE

SEAT

C1

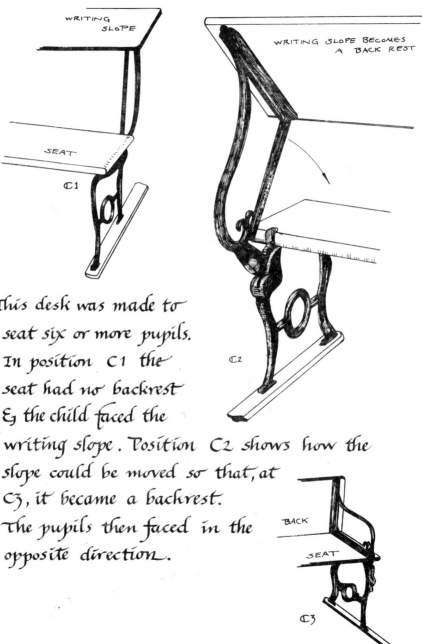

WRITING SLOPE BECOMES
A BACK REST

C2

This desk was made to seat six or more pupils. In position C1 the seat had no backrest & the child faced the writing slope. Position C2 shows how the slope could be moved so that, at C3, it became a backrest. The pupils then faced in the opposite direction.

BACK

SEAT

C3

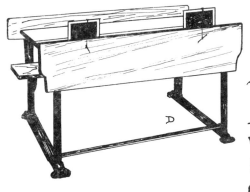

These dual desks probably appeared when the payments by results was banished in 1890.

Then the curriculum slowly changed as teachers developed their own more liberal ideas. Oak & cast iron were used for desks of this type. Example D has a lift-up seat & a writing slope. A slot was provided to hold slates when not in use. Example E has a slate rest below the slope.

This desk has more shelf space below the writing slope. There is an inkwell for each child & a pen groove to retain the pen. Cast iron & wood remained the basic materials until steel tubes replaced the ironwork in the 1920s.

Some desks had lockers like the example below.

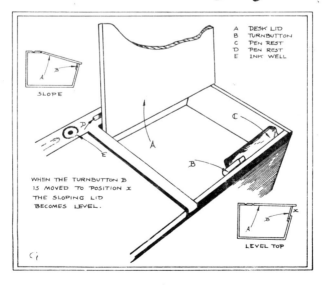

A	DESK LID
B	TURNBUTTON
C	PEN REST
D	PEN REST
E	INK WELL

SLOPE

WHEN THE TURNBUTTON B
IS MOVED TO POSITION x
THE SLOPING LID
BECOMES LEVEL.

LEVEL TOP

~THE TEACHER's DESK~

   In the Victorian schools the teacher was also the overseer of all the pupils. This supervisory element affected the design of furniture. The Teacher's desk & chair were high & the chair usually had a footrest.
Pupils visited the teacher's desk to have work marked & to be looked down upon by their mentor. The hand bell which ruled much of the school day was kept near the desk at the front of the class. This desk shows most of the common features. The teacher had two inkwells [A] for blue & red ink. Lift up shelves [B] were supported by hinged brackets [C].

The CANE D was usually kept in a visible place.
A cupboard E added to the desk's storage capacity.

A wooden CLICKER was
sometimes used by a teacher
to call a class to attention.

These interesting objects were sold by suppliers like E.J.
ARNOLD of Leeds & still appeared in catalogues in
the 1920s. As the slender trigger was squeezed it made
a loud click.

Teachers' chairs
of this kind were
made in High Wycombe
& were sold to many
local authorities.
There are several
variations to this
design ~ see
'COUNTRY SEATS'
in this series.

BLACKBOARDS~

A T-SQUARE WAS USED TO DRAW LINES ACROSS THE BOARD.

THIS BOARD COULD BE REVERSED BY REMOVING THE PIN x AT THE SIDE.

THE STAND MOVED ON CASTORS.

Blackboards & easles were essential elements of class furniture. Reading & singing charts could be fixed to the T-shaped slide [B] at [C]. The height of the board was adjusted by pegs [E].

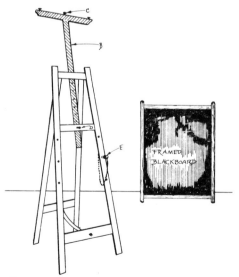

FRAMED BLACKBOARD

Postscript

In addition to the schools created by collective efforts, some individual donors were still establishing schools to serve their own parishes or estates in the C19. This example built by Mrs. Stackhouse Acton, in 1866, also had a teacher's house attached. At the rear the original 'offices' & a pig sty can still be seen. The presence of a sty tells us something about the teacher's social status. Flora Thompson ~ 'LARK RISE TO CANDLEFORD' ~ reminds us of the vicar's wife who was not sure if she should entertain the schoolmistress in the 'Kitchen or dining room.'!

From 1904 the County Council paid the teachers' salaries. The school closed in the 1980s. It now forms part of the Acton Scott Historic Working Farm, Shropshire.

This school was built in 1848 for the estate owner. The architect re-used masonry from a nearby church which was being renovated. The C13 turret which now surmounts the former chancel arch gives this building its unique profile. A C15 reredos forms one of the classroom walls. Miss Elizabeth Squire was the mistress here for a very long time - at least from 1891 until the school's closure in 1913. Classes can now visit to experience a Victorian school day. 'Miss Squire' again directs the lessons which enabled the country child to master the 3 R's.

DETAILS from Sevington School, SEVINGTON, Chippenham, WILTS, SN14 7LD.